# Living Adverbially

*poems by*

# Mike Wahl

*Finishing Line Press*
Georgetown, Kentucky

# Living Adverbially

Copyright © 2020 by Michael Wahl
ISBN 978-1-64662-156-9 First Edition
All rights reserved under International and Pan-American Copyright Conventions. No part of this book may be reproduced in any manner whatsoever without written permission from the publisher, except in the case of brief quotations embodied in critical articles and reviews.

## ACKNOWLEDGMENTS

I am deeply grateful to the greatest Benefactor who has enabled me to live in and enjoy my surroundings and circumstances, and for the words placed into my mind so rapidly that, at times, come so fast that the pen can't keep pace.

I would also like to thank the members of the Alabama State Poetry Society (ASPS) and those of the Huntsville Literary Association (HLA) poetry group who have encouraged my writing and provided constructive criticism when needed and when requested.

Publisher: Leah Maines
Editor: Christen Kincaid
Cover Art: *Living With the Bear Necessities* by Elisa Perry
Author Photo: Xerxes Wahl
Cover Design: Elizabeth Maines McCleavy

Printed in the USA on acid-free paper.
Order online: www.finishinglinepress.com
        also available on amazon.com

Author inquiries and mail orders:
Finishing Line Press
P. O. Box 1626
Georgetown, Kentucky 40324
U. S. A.

# Table of Contents

Introduction to the Book ................................................................. 1
Living Admirably ........................................................................... 2
Living Abruptly .............................................................................. 3
Living Abstractedly ....................................................................... 4
Living Adventurously .................................................................... 5
Living Abundantly ......................................................................... 6
Living Amphibiously ..................................................................... 7
Living Agreeably ............................................................................ 8
Living Abandonedly ...................................................................... 9
Living Astutely ............................................................................. 10
Living Adorably ........................................................................... 11
Living Accommodatingly ............................................................ 12
Living Abhorrently ...................................................................... 13
Living Absurdly ........................................................................... 14
Living Abysmally ......................................................................... 15
Living Atrociously ....................................................................... 16
Living Amorphously ................................................................... 17
Living Anticipatingly .................................................................. 18
Living Affectedly ......................................................................... 19
Living Aloofly .............................................................................. 20
Living Amicably .......................................................................... 21
Living Appropriately .................................................................. 22
Living Afterwards ....................................................................... 23
Living Anger-ally ........................................................................ 24
Living Abjectly ............................................................................ 25
Living Anguishingly ................................................................... 26
Living Appallingly ...................................................................... 27
Living Audaciously ..................................................................... 28
Living Avariciously ..................................................................... 29
Living Alternatively ................................................................... 30
Living Awarely ............................................................................ 31
Living Actuarially ....................................................................... 32
Living Acumen-ally .................................................................... 33
Living Awkwardly ...................................................................... 34
Living Always .............................................................................. 35
Living Apocalypticly ................................................................... 36

# Introducing the Book

Some poets think adverbs are overused in poems, but I happen to like the splash that adverbs add. Compromisingly, I set about to do something that would accentuate the concept of adverbs, without actually abusing them. So, that effort evolved into this collection. As with the title of the book, "Living Adverbially", each poem title is "Living (some adverb)", where those adverbs all begin with the letter "A" in homage to adverbs. Thus, the titles at least, are adverbial in nature. Thereby, maybe we can see if anyone else agrees with me about the deployment of adverbs in poetry.

Subjects of the poems include aspects of humor, insight, philosophy, politics, religion, and relationships. Pretty much anything goes, except I won't throw God under the bus. My preference is to write short poems with a succinct message or conclusion. This allows readers to laugh, snort in disgust, or nod in agreement, and then move on to the next page.

The poems, and especially the titles, tend to help explore the English language, and it may be necessary for the reader to occasionally look up a word. At times, I had to resort to that too, when searching for a word that began with "A" and still retained the overall gist of the poem. Some words/concepts don't have adverbial forms that are readily compatible, and that can make a title seem overbearing. I apologize for those times, and hope you will bear with me through the onslaught, knowing that I share your burden. I feel like I have been blessed to write poetry, but there are always new things and words to learn and use. By no means is there any intent to be pretentious, as I really want my words to be accessible to everyone, for enjoyment rather than for the interruption of a thought process because of an unfamiliar word. A "just get over it" attitude is detrimental, and I welcome any feedback that might help resolve such conflicts.

This is a long introduction for some short poems. Some rhyme, some don't. Some of you will love them, some won't. I hope you enjoy reading them as much as I delight in writing them.

**Living Admirably**


Intending tenacity,
the story stays more towards stubbornness,
favoring the shielded idiosyncrasies
until the desperation increases
enough to reveal
a satiated demon
dwelling within the confines
of an assigned absence,
causing a blushing,
and anchoring an apology.

**Living Abruptly**

When no one was watching,
the apple fell—
hard,
and although heretofore it had
no blemishes and no bugs,
it was now bruised and exposed,
made vulnerable by gravity,
and we get reminded of how
easily we all can fall
from the best sunlit branch
to the debasement of the ground,
even without gravity.

**Living Abstractedly**


I found Fastidious amongst my trash,
abandoned so many years ago
by purposeful misrepresentation,
then forgotten through misuse
and the abuse of dust in secret places.

Although at first I had missed Fastidious,
I never filed for a search or placed an ad,
and there were so many other
important things to do,
I just never had time to go looking.

I should have been reminded
of his absence by the films of dust
that wouldn't stay away,
but it was just so easy to ignore
what seemed so immaterially distant.

Since I have rediscovered Fastidious,
I now must decide if I want to
invite him to live with me again,
or just let that old stinky truck
haul him off to the dump, forever.

**Living Adventurously**

Can't call it a vacation,
since they are supposed
to be relaxing,
but at the very least, a journey.
Arduous is a good word, but really,
this experience went beyond that;
maybe somewhere between
frustrating and horrendous?
Way too much for the one,
but not quite enough for the other?

Considering the fumbled airline tickets,
the night in a foreign jail,
my back pocket being relieved
of credit cards, I.D., and money,
a most bizarre incident at the bazaar,
the false security breach at the Louvre—
Now, I love Paris,
but I won't ever go back,
so since it was my last visit,
where everything sure went sour,
let's just call it a lemonade adventure.

**Living Abundantly**

Overcoming an abundance
sometimes also overturns humility,
as Pride wedges itself between
a superseded Ego and Benevolence,
formulating an esoteric avenue where no one falls,
but the needle's eye gets even smaller,
and the marketplace somehow
manages to make a profit.

**Living Amphibiously**

Concentrically, the water announced
the entry of the frog,
where he had adeptly leapt,
barely escaping the
heron's reaching beak,
but still somehow, in mid air,
his instant instincts guided his
out-flung tongue to snag
the merest morsel of a mosquito.

And as he sank to the pond's bottom,
determined to just rest and digest,
at the surface,
waiting, wading, watching, wishing.

**Living Agreeably**

Picking through the fine hairs
of intended perfection,
someone finds a flaw—
but nits have no meaning
if you eat them, every one.
Friends can comb through
your every anticipation,
but until you can feature
an unrecognized reality,
be content to satisfy an itch
every now and then.

**Living Abandonedly**


The complexities of life
outwitted me again when they
overwhelmed my dedications,
outplayed my game,
out-spoke the diplomat,
overtook the leader,
inched incredibly up the incline,
overshadowed my best show,
uncorked the bottlenecks,
and then advertised with
complete abandonment
my inadequacies and failures.

**Living Astutely**

There was an accounting,
not necessarily in accordance
with normal accepted approaches,
rather, accommodating the meek and humble,
to accentuate the discrepancies of pride,
where barriers like the needle's eye
make accusations that uphold
the consequences of an ignored acuity.

**Living Adorably**

No words yet enable him,
but he knows the language well;
read to me—
he toddles to my chair,
clutching the small book,
as his one-year-old eyes say it best,
providing the combined punctuation
of a colon: an exclamation mark!
a beseeching question.
How can eyes so young simultaneously
convey his needs so effectively?
pleadingly; needingly;

No words yet enable him,
but he knows the lap and the soothing
voice that reads to him again,
the same exciting story of Peter Rabbit.

**Living Accommodatingly**

Please pretend that there's a place
tucked away inside a forgotten lock-box
where once there was a heart;
tell me words again that used to gush
*I love you, only you*
so we can put behind us any harshness,
and sink inside the horizon
where the sun knows no anger.

**Living Abhorrently**

Atrocities are a permanent reminder
of the degradation of mankind,
a devolvement into the holocausts
and genocides of a forlorn people,
not forgotten since their birthright
was stolen in the garden,
but abandoned by their own hopes
and forsaken by the interests of themselves.

**Living Absurdly**

Some say at arm's length
is sufficiently far away—
some would use a ten-foot pole,
and others into the next county;
I'm here to say that anything
detestable enough to be utterly avoided
is better served by
kicking the dirt off your sandals
and walking a mile in someone's shoes
that aren't quite so disgusting.

**Living Abysmally**


Steep are the hillsides of life,
rock-strewn and convoluted by the pits
and pocks of uncertainties and adversities,
where adversaries attack randomly
from behind emboldened boulders,
lubricating the slopes that advance
the dangling cliffs and cataclysmic cascades,
to keep us always at full alert
until fatigue finds us at nightfall,
vulnerable to the icy chill and moonless sky.

But to be lost in those foothills of depravity,
with more treacherous surrounding slopes
staring back, and no fruited plain in sight,
leaves a desperation of ultimate denial.

**Living Atrociously**

Perplexities, with unfound favor,
intertwine themselves into an already
complicated existence,
waiting for the proper opportunity
to exert the most atrocious
absurdities against the innocence
of unworthy guilt and the
fabrication of unbridled anxieties.

**Living Amorphously**

Normally castigated for his insolence
and apparent disregard for human favor,
he now groveled excessively to the magistrate
who held his freedom hostage,
and then they both had a chance
to ponder their positions
as they waited
while the wise man dreamt.

**Living Anticipatingly**
    *(where the grass grows greener)*

There is no pasture of lush longevity
where cows can graze up to infinity
if they were struck by that affinity,
instead of staring past their green vicinity
and over fences intended for exclusivity;

it is those barriers aligning their timidity
that also restrain the yearning of lustivity,
while making borders with a mighty inclinivity
to propose, perhaps there is another objectivity—
that the status quo is not complete depravity;

with insight might the cows show less proclivity
to jump a fence that leads into a vast obscurity—
if they could recognize rewards of their stability,
and honestly admit a lack of proper selectivity,
and thus avoid the weedy places advocating inability.

Embracing the notions of abiding secretivity,
brings disregard for boundaries curtailing flexibility,
and ignoring implications of benefits withheld for ingenuity;
indeed, folly would lead to mere boundaries of nebulosity,
where the grass has the same greenness as ubiquity.

(the other side of the fence is nonexistent)

**Living Affectedly**

We wonder at the confusion
of mixed accountabilities,
slung without due concern
against an assortment
of wishful thinking,
then blinking back the tide
of an upsurging
renaissance of realization
that false truths
have their own consequences,
we ponder what's left
of an unrehearsed configuration.

**Living Aloofly**

We wondered about the hill
that wasn't there yesterday,
and about the mountain we thought
we might be enabled to move,
so that with heightened expectations,
we then supposed the insignificance
of molehills made walking on flat ground
an easy prospect for a level tomorrow,
never realizing that sinking was an option.

**Living Amicably**

To pierce the golden sky,
previously unfolded,
boldly, and unannounced,
with unforetold consequences—
to cleverly divide the mossy ledge
where stalactites part their ways—
to regain the ground, elsewhere,
also unannounced,
then fleeing,
while trying to catch the essence
of the piercing of the sky.

**Living Appropriately**

Bygones should be just that,
not stuck in some nearby niche
within easy reaching,
waiting to be pulled out
with enough provocation,
then dusted off and even enhanced
with a ritzy word or two,
to be flaunted to the world;
no, bygones should be

**Living Afterwards**


Before there were cell phones,
there was you,
but you never called.

Before there was color,
there was black and white,
but you were a monotone of gray.

Before Samson knew Delilah,
there was strength,
but I told you all my secrets.

While the seven dwarfs fussed as you slept,
the prince came kissing,
but it wasn't me.

Once the poet wrote your poem
to offer to the world,
but you too rejected it.

**Living Anger-ally**

Hanging on,
(past the edge,
past that boundary we would say was reason,
to encounter that world illogically,
and to revel in its existence,
in a realm of catacombs and recesses
where excuses hide randomly
beside the disguised
but abused truth,)
is you,
abiding in your stubborn dungeon.

**Living Abjectly**

These are the tortured trials
of a non-abundant existence
that harbor the resentments
and the hatred of in-grown spirits,
thus leading to an otherwise early demise.
Ignorance, not being bliss, is not recognized.
Mobs form.
They hold common sense as hostage.
No one pays the ransom.
It's the same game we keep playing,
and no one ever wins, not even the house.

## Living Anguishingly

The boat slid silently through the waves
with her sails silhouetted against
the western reds and oranges,
leaving me alone with a singular
circle of sand surrounding one
forlorn thought of a forgotten tree.
How could I survive the thirst,
first of all, and if that, the hunger?
My bag was packed with only attitudes
and abandoned eagles' flights,
instead of flashlights, first aid kits,
or sunscreens.

The first dawn was cool,
giving me hope that my
sanity might stay longer—
until the tumbling bottle
escaped the surf to land at my feet,
revealing its message that
there was no ticket office
or shipping lane nearby.

## Living Appallingly

It was our last chance to say
*I love you* to someone who wasn't there,
and then the bombs fell,
so we could no longer speak
against the atrocities of war,
but our bones will testify
until the twilight dwindles
into total chaos.

**Living Audaciously**

Was it a one-night stand?
We took the existence
of an unproven protocol
as a negotiable opportunity
to overcome the resistance
blocking a carefree night
that had yielded to persistence.

There were no witnesses
and no sirens, except in the distance,
when we robbed the bank at 2:00 AM;
a cash withdrawal
was our single insistence.

**Living Avariciously**

INGREDIENTS FOR GREED:
start with a large bowl
(a very large bowl) of ego—
use the all-purpose kind,
but add a generous sprinkling of
'it's all about me' to it anyway;
add a heaping cup of selfishness and
three large portions of pride—
blend these together in the bowl and set aside.
(exercise caution, as it may resist being set aside)
In a large skillet, add all the money you can find,
plus paid-off mortgage notes,
deeds to properties,
and titles to vehicles;
stir together well while sauteing
until it is filthy rich.
Haphazardly mix together
the ingredients of the skillet and bowl
until the stench gets so bad
you have to leave the country.

**Living Alternatively**

You disappear inside the categories
you were sent to salvage;
file folders found empty;
projects passed to interns
who know no history;
embezzlements against the holdings
already stretched into the red;
zones of nonchalance that should
have had more barrier tape instead;
at the consultation you say again
you'll do better, but after you have left,
my pen and pad of notes are also gone.

**Living Awarely**

I am a decrepit old man,
gnarled of persona
that matches arthritic
fingers and knees,
keenly aware that the
vast void arrays itself
behind the curtains
of certain detachment
in the black segments
of unfolded time.

**Living Actuarially**

There are the theories and the promises
of living long and staying strong,
but none will much prevail.

There are the mystical statistics
describing normals and averages
for each of us to assail.

The overdone opinions and skewed views
can't outdo the labors and sorrows of Psalm 90,
where reaching eighty makes us frail;

so, if a man exceeds today's life expectancy,
should it count if one has to feel twice
for signs of life's last faltering detail?

## Living Acumen-ally

Initially, there was no clue
that the pathway was forked.
Someone suggested that
we all dive in, naked.
I went for the ice-cream,
colder than the pool,
and so much more enticing
in the summer heat;
I came to the pool routinely
every evening to wash away
the dust of weeds
and cotton and bugs,
knowing sleep was close behind.

But the ice-cream was in
a dream world of its own,
and my mama said it would
one day inherit the earth,
along with the chosen few.

**Living Awkwardly**


Perhaps it is an awkwardness
that thrusts itself inside the threshold
I had tried to keep secure,
a boundary beyond which is meant
to be only mine, undefiled;

reviled is that awkwardness,
so unkempt and unlike my other thoughts;
meanwhile, the postcards keep on coming,
and the letters offer suggestions
that are meaningless—

if I can find a place that
better accommodates my ways,
one that can invigorate intrepidity,
I will fight in its defense,
and arrange to live there evermore.

**Living Always**

TO BE like an infinitive;
an existence that equates definitive
diligence to truth held constant,
and captive never to the non-divinities,
who seek towards a relief of sympathy
instead of adherence to confession,
leaving grace in a corner unattended,
but free to approach infinity
inside the unbounded mercy of
a reconciled realization
that TO BE is I AM.

**Living Apocalypticly**

Nation against nation bleeds too fast,
as do hurricanes and tornadoes,
their winds blowing rain and floods
into the lives that are left.
Is it really a choice,
to die in battle or by wind?
The winds grow more fierce every year—
it is the coming time.
The nations battle into Armageddon
for the final fling.
Winds won't matter anymore.

www.ingramcontent.com/pod-product-compliance
Lightning Source LLC
LaVergne TN
LVHW041556070426
835507LV00011B/1107